A LOOK AT U.S. HISTORY

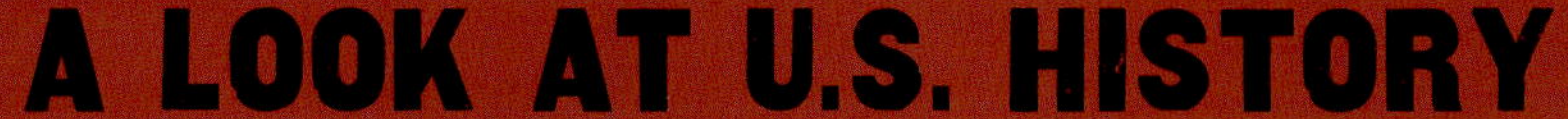

PRIMARIES AND CAUCUSES

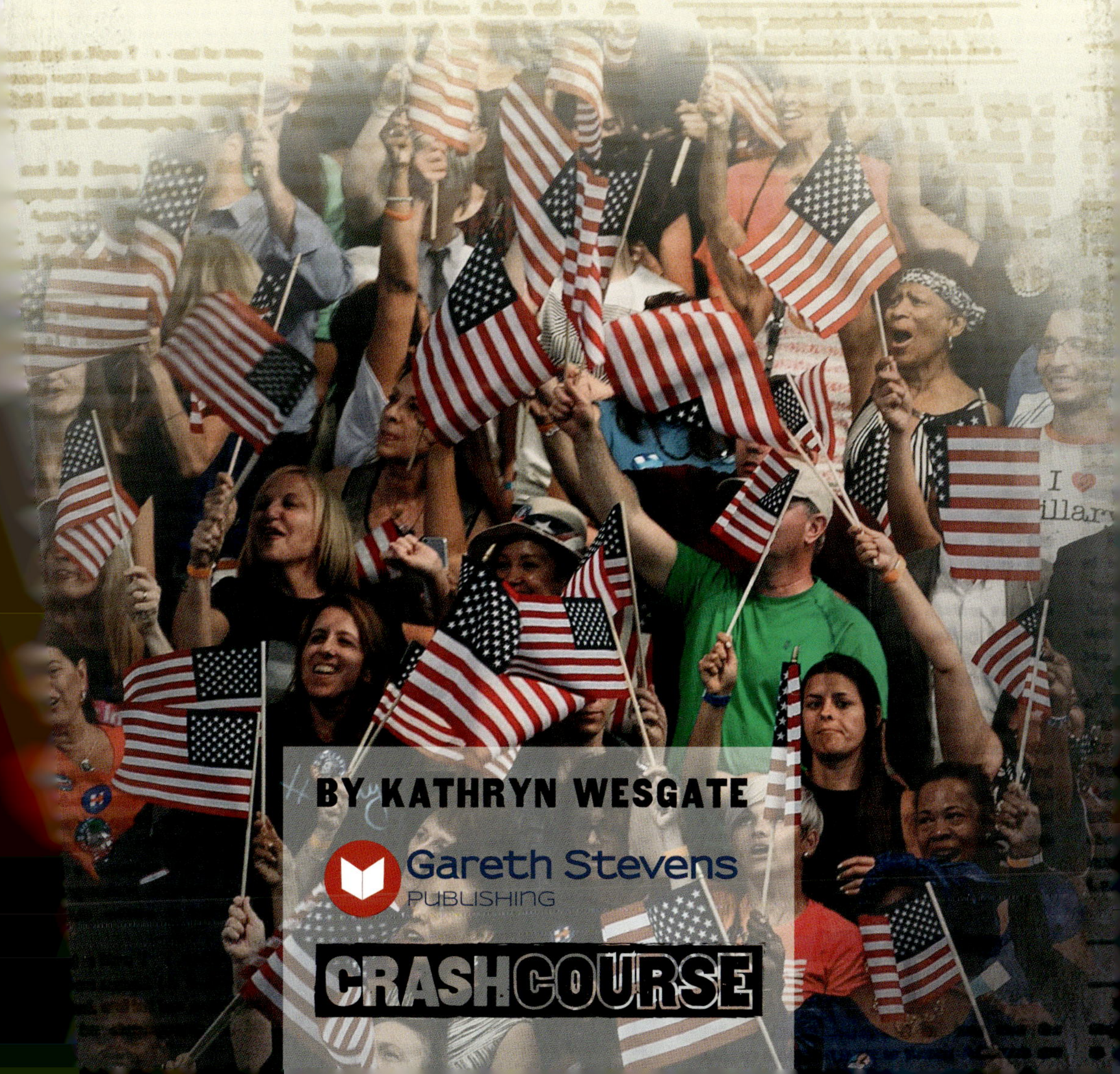

BY KATHRYN WESGATE

Gareth Stevens PUBLISHING

CRASHCOURSE

Please visit our website, www.garethstevens.com. For a free color catalog of all our high-quality books, call toll free 1-800-542-2595 or fax 1-877-542-2596.

Library of Congress Cataloging-in-Publication Data
Names: Wesgate, Kathryn, author.
Title: Primaries and caucuses / Kathryn Wesgate.
Description: New York : Gareth Stevens Publishing, [2021] | Series: A look at U.S. elections | Includes index. | Contents: Choosing the candidates -- Party time! -- Road to the White House -- Primary or caucus? -- Primary time -- Open and closed -- Caucuses -- Super Tuesday -- Important Elections.
Identifiers: LCCN 2019054539 | ISBN 9781538259566 (library binding) | ISBN 9781538259542 (paperback) | ISBN 9781538259559 (6 Pack) | ISBN 9781538259573 (ebook)
Subjects: LCSH: Primaries--United States--Juvenile literature. | Caucus--United States--Juvenile literature. | Presidents--United States--Nomination--Juvenile literature. | Presidents--United States--Election--Juvenile literature. | United States--Politics and government--Juvenile literature.
Classification: LCC JK2071 .W47 2021 | DDC 324.273/15--dc23
LC record available at https://lccn.loc.gov/2019054539

First Edition

Published in 2021 by
Gareth Stevens Publishing
111 East 14th Street, Suite 349
New York, NY 10003

Editor: Kate Mikoley

Photo credits: Cover, p. 1 Drew Angerer/Getty Images News/Getty Images; series art kzww/Shutterstock.com; series art (newspaper) MaryValery/Shutterstock.com; pp. 5, 7, 13, 19, 23 Hill Street Studios/DigitalVision/Getty Images; pp. 9, 17, 29 Hero Images/Getty Images; p. 11 Mike Mergen/Bloomberg/Getty Images; p. 15 Digital Vision./DigitalVision/Getty Images; p. 21 Robert Alexander/Archive Photos/Getty Images; p. 25 MICHAEL B. THOMAS /AFP/Getty Images; p. 27 https://commons.wikimedia.org/wiki/File:Super_Tuesday_Ballots_in_Massachusetts.jpg.

Printed in the United States of America

CPSIA compliance information: Batch #CS20GS: For further information contact Gareth Stevens, New York, New York at 1-800-542-2595.

CONTENTS

Words in the glossary appear in **bold** type the first time they are used in the text.

CHOOSING THE CANDIDATES

You might already know that an election is the act of voting someone into a government position. The **final** election that decides a winner is called the general election. Before a general election, **candidates** are chosen. This is where primaries and caucuses come in.

Make the Grade

General elections, such as the presidential election, commonly take place in November. Primaries and caucuses happen months earlier.

PARTY TIME!

A political party is a group of people with **similar** beliefs and ideas about government. These parties work to have their members elected to government offices. In the United States, the Democratic and Republican parties are the two main political parties.

Make the Grade

Primaries and caucuses are events that let political parties choose which candidates they want to run for their party in a general election.

ROAD TO THE WHITE HOUSE

The most well-known general election in the United States is the presidential election. This happens every four years. The most famous primaries and caucuses are held before this election, although primaries and caucuses both happen at other times too.

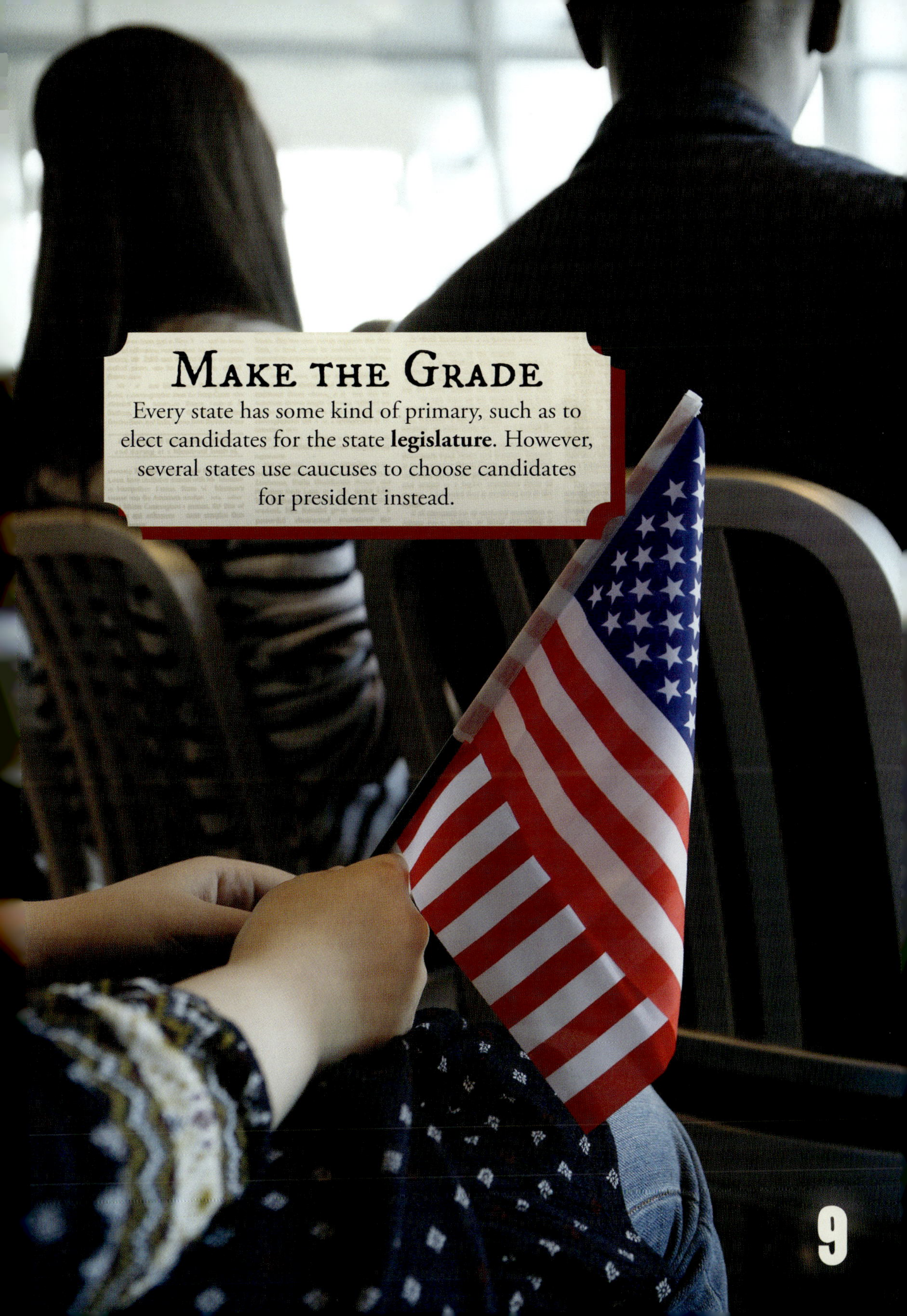

Make the Grade

Every state has some kind of primary, such as to elect candidates for the state **legislature**. However, several states use caucuses to choose candidates for president instead.

Before presidential elections, both main parties have an event called the national **convention**. Primaries and caucuses choose who gets to go to these conventions for each state. At the conventions, chosen members vote for the candidate they want to **represent** their party.

Make the Grade

The people chosen to go to their party's national convention and vote for a candidate are called delegates.

PRIMARY OR CAUCUS?

Primaries are elections run by the government. People's votes are kept secret, unless they choose to tell someone. Caucuses are meetings run by political parties. At caucuses, people talk about the different candidates before a vote is taken.

Make the Grade

In early U.S. history, presidential candidates were chosen mainly through caucuses. Today, primaries are more common.

PRIMARY TIME

A primary is an election where voters pick which candidate from a political party they want to run in the general election. The winner gets the support, or backing, of their party to run against the other parties' candidates.

Make the Grade

When a party picks a person to run for an office, it's called nominating. The person chosen is called a nominee.

Before a party chooses a candidate, there are often many in the running. They **campaign** and take part in debates, or events where several candidates **discuss** and argue their ideas. Some candidates from debates go on to run in the primaries.

Make the Grade

Debates are often shown on TV. Watching them can be a good way to get to know which candidates you agree with.

OPEN AND CLOSED

The **U.S. Constitution** gave states control over how to run elections. This means each state can run their primaries a little differently. Open and closed primaries are the two basic kinds, but some states have different rules and methods.

Make the Grade

Your state's primaries may be a little different than regular open or closed primaries. Ask a trusted adult to help you find out how primaries work where you live!

Voters commonly agree more often with one party than another. They may be registered, or signed up, to vote with that party. In a closed primary, voters can only vote for a candidate from the party they're in.

Make the Grade

Some voters choose not to register with a party. These people can't vote in closed primaries.

In an open primary, anyone who can vote is allowed to pick which party's primary they want to take part in. They can vote for any candidate they choose. It doesn't matter which party the voter or the candidate belongs to.

Make the Grade

Some states let voters who haven't registered with a party vote for any candidate in primaries, but those who have must choose someone from their own party.

CAUCUSES

Like primaries, caucuses can be open, closed, or a mix of both. These party-run meetings are most commonly held to pick delegates who go on to vote for candidates to run for president. However, caucuses can be held to decide on other **issues** too.

Make the Grade

The most famous caucuses in the United States are the Iowa caucuses. They're commonly the first caucuses or primaries held before a presidential election.

SUPER TUESDAY

Super Tuesday is a day when many states hold their primaries or caucuses. It's commonly in March. This is a big day because candidates have the chance to win the votes of many delegates from many states.

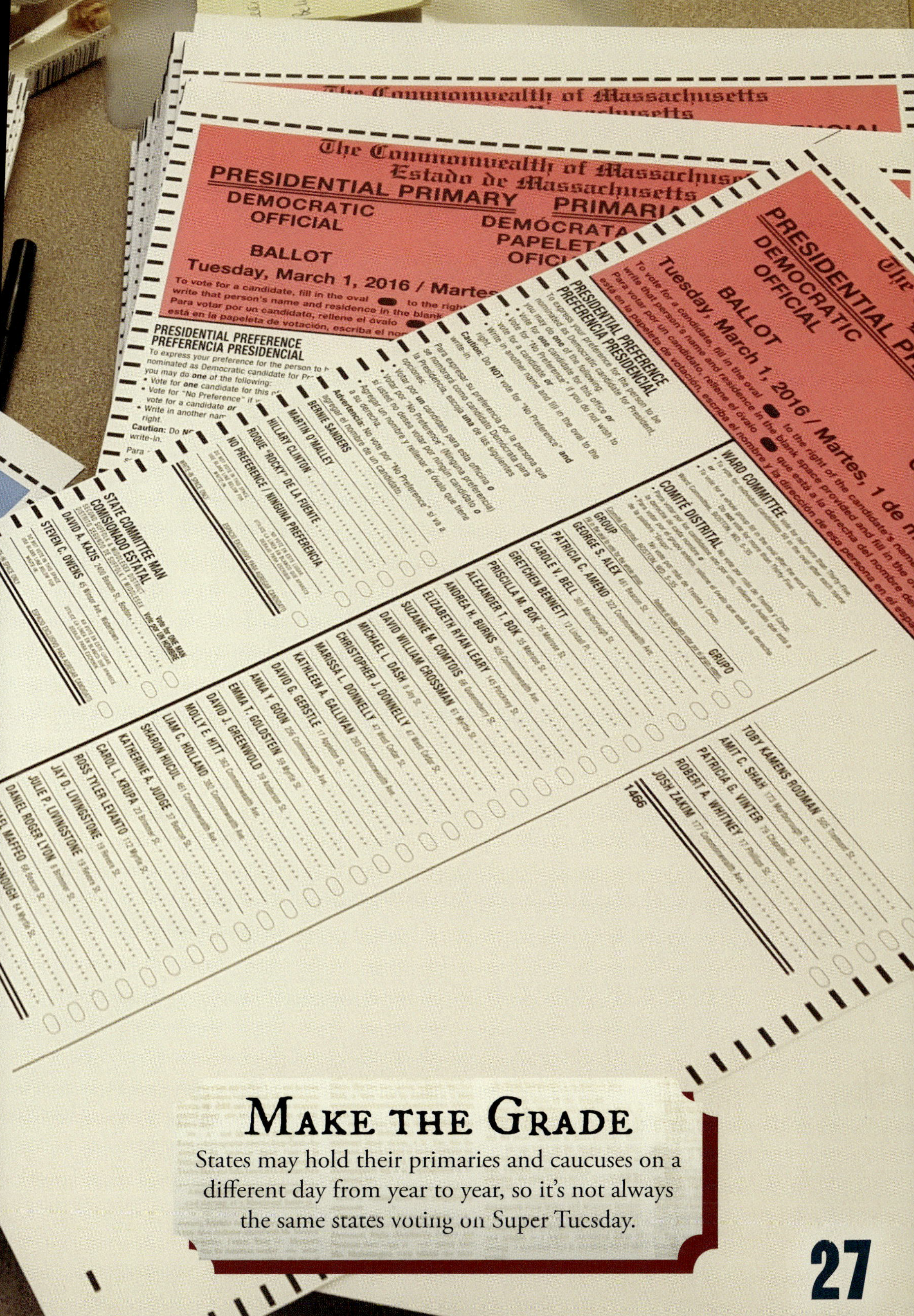

Make the Grade

States may hold their primaries and caucuses on a different day from year to year, so it's not always the same states voting on Super Tuesday.

IMPORTANT ELECTIONS

The general election often gets all the attention. This seems to be even more true during presidential election years. But primaries and caucuses are important too! After all, these are the events that decide who actually runs in the general election.

Make the Grade

You have to be 18 to vote, but you can start getting ready now. Pay attention to candidates and elections now, and you'll be more prepared when you're older!

COMPARING PRIMARIES AND CAUCUSES

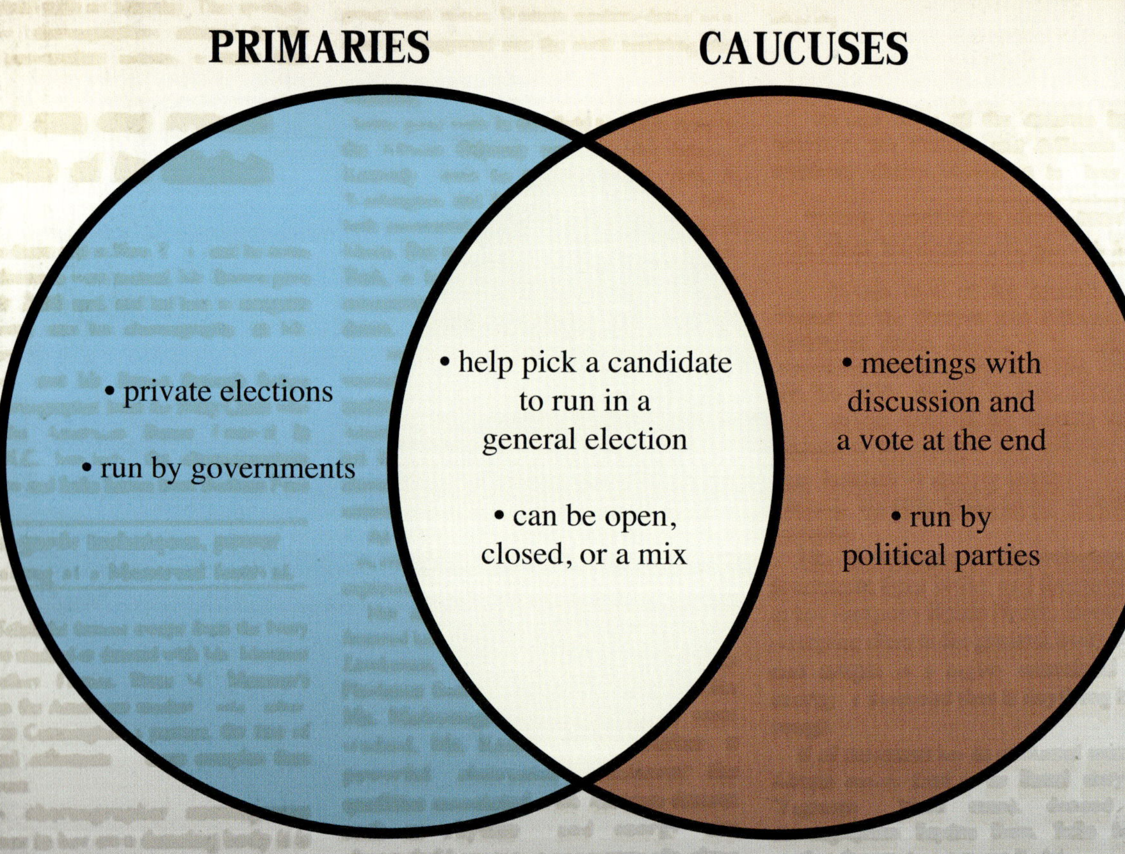

GLOSSARY

campaign: to do activities to try to get people to support something or vote for a candidate

candidate: a person who is running for office

convention: a gathering of people who have a common interest or purpose

discuss: to talk about something

final: the last of something in a series, or group, of things that happen

issue: an important subject that people are talking or thinking about

legislature: a lawmaking body

represent: to stand for. A person who represents is a representative.

similar: almost the same as something else

U.S. Constitution: the piece of writing that states the laws of the United States

FOR MORE INFORMATION

BOOKS

Conley, Kate. *Voting and Elections*. Minneapolis, MN: Core Library, an imprint of ABDO Publishing, 2017.

Grayson, Robert. *Voters: From Primaries to Decision Night*. Minneapolis, MN: Lerner Publishing Group, 2016.

WEBSITES

Government 101: United States Presidential Primary
votesmart.org/education/presidential-primary
Find out more about the presidential primary process here.

How Voting Works
www.ducksters.com/history/us_government_voting.php
Find out more about how voting works on this website.

Publisher's note to educators and parents: Our editors have carefully reviewed these websites to ensure that they are suitable for students. Many websites change frequently, however, and we cannot guarantee that a site's future contents will continue to meet our high standards of quality and educational value. Be advised that students should be closely supervised whenever they access the internet.

INDEX

A LOOK AT U.S. ELECTIONS

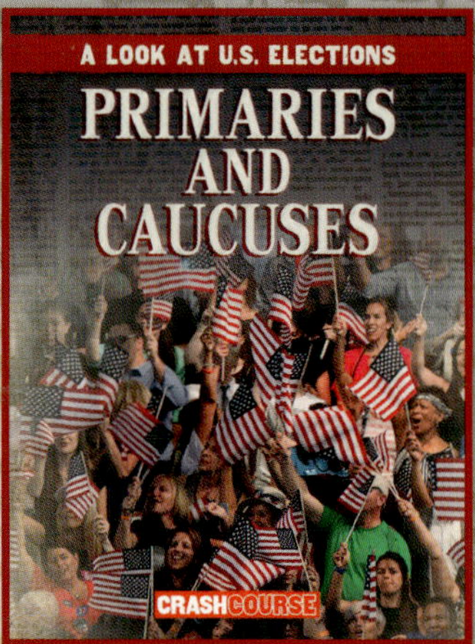

ISBN: 9781538259542
6-pack ISBN: 9781538259559
9 781538 259542

WORDS THAT SHAPED AMERICA

THE MOST POWERFUL WORDS ABOUT THE AMERICAN DREAM

LIFE, LIBERTY, and the PURSUIT of HAPPINESS.

CAITIE McANENEY